Holy Week for Children

Written by Michele E. Chronister
Illustrated by Michele and Therese Chronister
©2018

©2019 All rights reserved. No part of this book may be reproduced without permission, except for the coloring pages (which may be reproduced for personal use only).

Genre: [Catholic Liturgy] [Catechesis] [Easter]
Summary: A glimpse at what a child will see at the liturgies of Holy Week in the Catholic Church.

ISBN-13: 978-1986269872

Another My Domestic Monastery publication. For more info, visit: http://www.mydomesticmonastery.com

Icons in this book are a study of classic icons depicting the Scriptural stories, incorporating the traditional elements of each icon.

Special thanks to Therese Chronister, age 7, for her original icon of the resurrection included with the closing prayer.

Dedicated in memory of Gabriel Chronister, who spent his short time on earth celebrating Holy Week with me.

It's Holy Week.

What do we remember?

What will you see?

It's **Palm Sunday**.

What do we remember?

We remember when **Jesus entered Jerusalem on a donkey**. The people waved palms and shouted, "HOSANNA!"

What will you see?

You will see the priest **bless the palms**.

You may see the people **process with the palms**.

You will hear the **story of the first Palm Sunday,** and the **story of Jesus's Passion and Death**.

It's **Holy Thursday**.

It is the beginning of the **Sacred Triduum** – Holy Thursday, Good Friday, and Holy Saturday (the Easter Vigil).

What do we remember?

We remember the **Last Supper**, when Jesus gave us the gift of the **priesthood**, and the gift of the **Eucharist**, His Body and Blood.

What will you see?

In the morning, there is a special liturgy called the **Chrism Mass.**

It is held at the **cathedral** and celebrated by the **bishop** and **all the priests** of the diocese.
It is a special Mass that celebrates the priesthood, since Jesus made the Apostles the first priests at the Last Supper.

You will also see the bishop bless the **Oil of the Sick** (for the Anointing of the Sick), and the **Oil of Catechumens** (for Baptisms).

The bishop will also mix and consecrate the **Sacred Chrism Oil**. This oil is used at Baptisms, Ordinations, and Confirmations.

The priests will take these oils back to each of their parishes, to use for the Sacraments throughout the year.

In the evening, there is the **Mass of the Lord's Supper**. It is held at your parish. It is the first liturgy of the Sacred Triduum.

The oils that were blessed and consecrated are carried up to the altar.

The readings tell the story of the Last Supper, when Jesus first turned the bread into His Body and the wine into His Blood. The Gospel tells the story of when Jesus washed the feet of His Apostles.

After the homily, **the priest washes the feet of twelve people** in the parish, to remind us of when Jesus washed the feet of His Apostles.

There is no closing blessing at the end of the Mass. That is because the Mass doesn't really end – the liturgies of the Triduum are just one long liturgy. Because of this, there will not be a closing blessing until the end of the Easter Vigil.

Instead of the closing blessing, there is a **procession to the Altar of Repose**. Instead of putting Jesus in the Eucharist into the main tabernacle, the priest carries him to a special side tabernacle. There is incense. There are candles. All are invited to stay and pray.

The **Altar of Repose** is decorated like a garden, to remind us of when Jesus went to the Garden of Gethsemane to pray. Like he invited the Apostles, he invites us to stay and pray with him awhile.

It is **Good Friday**.

What do we remember?

We remember when **Jesus died on the cross**.

There is no Mass on Good Friday, just a special service called the **Celebration of the Passion of the Lord**.

What will you see?

The altar is bare. The tabernacle is empty. **The priest enters in silence** and lays on the ground to pray.

You will hear **the story of the Passion and Death of Jesus.**

You will pray the **Solemn Intercessions**, the special prayers for all the people in the Church and the people in the whole world.

You will get to participate in the **Adoration of the Holy Cross**. The priest or deacon will carry the cross to the altar. Then, each person may come to the cross and kiss it. This is called **venerating the cross**.

We kiss the cross, because it is a reminder of God's great love for us. Some churches may even have a relic, or a tiny piece of Jesus's real cross. This relic may be placed inside a larger cross for veneration.

Although it is not a Mass, there is still an opportunity for people to receive Jesus in the Eucharist, before the end of the service.
All leave in silence.

It's **Holy Saturday.**

What do we remember?

We remember when **Jesus's body laid in the tomb.**

We also remember when **Jesus descended to the dead.** When Jesus died on the cross, he opened the gates to heaven.

Before he died on the cross, all the holy men and women who had died had to wait to enter heaven.

On Holy Saturday, Jesus freed them and led them to heaven. This picture shows him leading Adam and Eve to heaven.

In the evening, the celebration of Jesus's resurrection will begin.

What will you see?

Holy Saturday is a day of **quiet and waiting.**

The church is being decorated for Easter, and your family may be finishing preparing for your own celebration.

Some parishes may pray **Morning Prayer** and do the **Blessing of the Easter Foods.**

Families bring baskets of the food that they will eat for their Easter meal. The priest blesses the food.

In the evening, there is the Easter Vigil.

The Easter Vigil is a long, very beautiful Mass. It is made up of four parts –
the Liturgy of Light,
the Liturgy of the Word,
the Liturgy of Baptism, and
the Liturgy of the Eucharist.

The Mass begins with the Liturgy of Light.

Outside the church, the priest lights a special fire, called the Paschal fire. The Paschal candle is blessed and lit from the fire. The Paschal candle represents Jesus Christ, who is our light.

The candle is carried into a dark church. Each person is given a candle, and the candles are then lit from the light of the Paschal candle.

This special candle will be used at Baptisms and funerals all year long and will be lit at every Mass of the Easter season. After the priest or deacon processes into the church with the Paschal candle, the Exsultet is sung by candlelight. The special song tells of how this Easter night is truly wondrous.

The **Liturgy of the Word** is next.

At an ordinary Sunday Mass, there are only three readings. At the Easter Vigil, there may be as many as **nine readings**. This is because the readings tell the story of salvation history.

Salvation history is the story of how God saved his people from sin and opened the way to heaven.

The readings begin with the story of creation. They also include the stories of Abraham, Moses, and the prophets. The **Gloria** and the **Alleluia** are sung, and bells are rung. The final reading is the story of Jesus's resurrection in the Gospel. The resurrection of Jesus is what all the people of the Old Testament were waiting for!

The Liturgy of Baptism follows the readings.

During the Liturgy of Baptism, all the older children and adults who have been preparing to enter the Church are baptized. These are the **Catechumens**. Adults who are baptized this night also receive the Sacrament of Confirmation at the Easter Vigil.

Some older children and adults have already been baptized in churches that are not Catholic, but that are also Christian. These are the **Candidates for Full Communion**. To enter the Church, they just pray a special prayer, and are not baptized again.

All children and adults who have already been baptized renew their **Baptismal promises** on this night. They promise to reject the devil, follow Jesus, and profess everything that the Church teaches. All are then **blessed with holy water** by the priest, as a reminder of their baptism. Some churches may not have any baptisms at the Easter Vigil. All will still renew their Baptismal promises and be blessed with holy water. Mass ends with the **Liturgy of the Eucharist**, and a closing blessing.

It's **Easter Sunday**.

What do we remember?

We remember when **Jesus rose from the dead** on the third day.

We remember how Jesus defeated sin and death and opened the gates of heaven.

Those who did not attend the Easter Vigil will go to Mass on Easter Sunday. Some people may go to both.

With the Easter Vigil begins the great season of celebrating in the Church. For the next fifty days, we will celebrate the Resurrection of Jesus from the dead.

The week after Holy Week is the **Octave of Easter**. For eight days, every day is celebrated with as much joy and celebration as Easter Sunday.

Christ is risen.

Truly he is risen!

-traditional Easter greeting

(right: an original icon of the resurrection by Therese Chronister, age 7)

Icons

(The following pages contain icons that can be cut out and used around your home or classroom, to assist in your family's prayer and reflection during Holy Week. Please do not make copies of them.)

Coloring Pages

(The following coloring pages may be reproduced for personal use only, i.e. in the classroom, home, or parish.)

Made in the USA
Coppell, TX
29 March 2020